Dag Heward-Mills

strategies
for
Prayer

Copyright © 2008
Lux Verbi.BM (Pty) Ltd, PO Box 5, Wellington 7654, South Africa
Tel +27 21 864 8200
www.luxverbi-bm.com
Reg no 1953/000037/07
1st Printing 2008

E mail Dag Heward-Mills :
bishop@daghewardmills.org
evangelist@daghewardmills.org

Find out more about Dag Heward-Mills at:
www.daghewardmills.org
www.lighthousechapel.org
www.healingjesuscrusade.org

Write to:
Dag Heward-Mills
P.O. Box 114
Korle-Bu
Accra
Ghana

ISBN 13: 978-0-7963-0817-7

Contents

Chapter 1

Daniel's Principles of Prayer

Now when Daniel knew that the writing was signed, he went into his house; and his windows being open in his chamber toward Jerusalem, he kneeled upon his knees three times a day, and prayed, and gave thanks before his God, as he did aforetime.

Daniel 6:10

Y ou will notice from this Scripture that Daniel prayed three times a day. An important phrase used in this verse is "as he did aforetime". That means that Daniel had been praying these prayers on a regular basis. Daniel was not just praying because he was in trouble; he had a habit of praying.

Many times when people become prosperous they stop going for prayer meetings and eventually backslide. Not so with Daniel! He was the Prime Minister of his country, second in authority only to the king. He was a successful man who had risen from slavery to the high office of Prime Minister. He was one of the most respected and feared men in the nation. He was a major politician of the day. He was a civil servant. Yet, he prayed three times a day, *everyday*!

What were the principles that guided Daniel to have such an unusual and consistent prayer time? Here they are, read them and let them become *your* principles. You too can have the success that Daniel had. I want you to read through, study and analyze the following principles that I believe guided Daniel in his life.

Principle No. 1: Prayer Is Very Important

Someone once said that it is more important to know how to pray than to have a degree from the university. There are many things that are important in this life. A good education is important. Money is important. A good marriage is important. But, *a good prayer life is most important!*

Let this enter your spirit—*In all your getting, get prayer!* In all your activities, make room for prayer!

Principle No. 2: No One Is Ever Too Busy, Too Blessed or Too Successful to Pray

You may have a busy life style and you may be a very important person, however; I do not think that you are busier than Daniel was. Daniel was a Prime Minister, a leader in the nation. Many people think that Heads of State and Ministers of government have a relaxed and enjoyable life, flying all over the world. That is not true! I am the head of a large organization myself, and I know that people in high positions do not have an easy life. **The higher you go, the greater the responsibility you have.**

There is so much hard work involved in staying on the cutting edge of life and ministry. Did you know that successful executives like Daniel are so stressed out that they are prone to diseases like stomach ulcers and heart attacks? These conditions are more common with very busy people because of the hard work that they do.

Daniel was one such person. He was a Prime Minister, yet he felt that he was not too busy to pray three times a day. **If you think you are too busy to pray, then you are deceiving yourself.** If you do not pray, it is because you do not want to pray. It is because you do not think that prayer is important now! Daniel was successful, yet he prayed. Why was he able to pray three times a day?

I have watched people in the church rise out of poverty into mega blessings. When they were poor, they had a lot of time to attend prayer meetings. But when they became blessed, they felt everything was all right. No! Everything is not all right! **Your state of blessing is not the signal to stop praying.**

Principle No. 3: Prayer is the Source of Our Power and Protection

You must realize that it is prayer which releases the power of God on our behalf. Jesus knew the power of prayer. That is why he spent long hours in prayer.

Maybe you are a successful businessman, and you do not think that you need any of this spiritual "stuff". Perhaps you are a politician and you think your protection must come from fetish or occult powers.

Let me tell you right now, there is power in prayer. We do not need any other power when we have the power of prayer. There is protection for us when we pray. The last part of the armour of God is prayer (Ephesians 6:18). In other words, prayer is an important part of your spiritual defence.

In Ghana, many people become afraid when they prosper. They feel that somebody may use supernatural powers to try to kill them. You have nothing to fear when you are a prayerful person like Daniel.

Many people wanted to kill Daniel. These people did not just think about killing Daniel, they actually plotted to eliminate him. Through the power of prayer, Daniel was protected from the lions.

I see all the lions in your life scattering away in fear! I see your prayer power rising! I see you going forward because of a new found prayer life!

...that Jesus also being baptized, and praying, the Heaven was opened.

Luke 3:21

I see the Heavens opening over your life! Never forget this! The Heavens opened when Jesus prayed. *Both physical and spiritual blessings rain upon you when you are a prayerful person.*

Principle No. 4: Prayer is Important in Acquiring and Sustaining the Blessings of God

Do you have anything that you are proud of? Have you achieved anything in this life? Let me tell you that it is by the grace of God. By the power of prayer, you will achieve many greater things. It is by prayer that you will sustain what God has placed in your hands.

I know of people who were given thousands of dollars as gifts. Today, that money has disappeared into thin air. God may give you something but it also takes His grace to sustain that blessing. Are you the pastor of a great ministry? Let me tell you, it takes prayer to sustain you in the ministry. Why do you think Jesus kept running away to pray?

There is a law of degeneration at work in the world. Everything is decaying. Your business is decaying. Your church is decaying. Your very life is decaying. It takes the power of God, through prayer, to preserve everything that God has given to you.

Pinciple No. 5: For Prayer to Be Effective it Must Be Habitual

A man called Dostoyevsky said, "The second half of a man's life is made up of the habits he acquired in the first half."

Pascal said, "The strength of a man's virtues is made up of his habitual acts."

If you are going to be a great person in this life, you need to have good habits. An action becomes a habit when

5

it is repeated many times; sometimes consciously, other times unconsciously. It becomes your custom!

Habits can be either good or bad. Remember that good habits are repeated as easily as bad habits. A good habit will lead to consistent breakthroughs even without intending to. Bad habits will also lead to consistent failure. If you decide to develop a habit of prayer, you are developing a habit for success.

Jesus went to church on the Sabbath because it was his habit. The Bible tells us that Jesus had customs or habits.

...as his custom [habit] **was, he went into the synagogue on the sabbath day...**

Luke 4:16

Daniel had a custom of praying three times a day.

...he [Daniel] **kneeled upon his knees three times a day, and prayed...**

Daniel 6:10

Life in the secular world is not designed to include a prayer time. Work starts early in the morning and continues late into the night. Weeks may pass before you even think of prayer. For many people, it is only an impossible situation that reminds them of the need for prayer. Dear friend, it is important for you to include prayer in your life.

God is not a spare tyre! A spare tyre is something that is never used except in emergencies. God is no fool. Whatsoever a man sows, he will reap. If you have time for God on a regular basis, He will have time to bless you on a regular basis. Only the mercy of God makes Him listen to some of our prayers.

Develop your prayer life until it happens spontaneously. Develop your prayer life until you pray habitually without even thinking of what you are doing.

I Made Time to Pray

When I was a medical student, I was very busy with my coursework. There was no time to pray at all. But because I had made prayer a part of my Christian life, there was no way I could do without it! I had to somehow include it in my schedule. I decided to pray late at night. I was usually so sleepy that I had to walk about just to stay awake. Prayer was so important to me that I could not leave it out of my life.

One night, as I headed for my room after one of such prayer times, I actually fell asleep whilst walking! It was only when I walked into the Spanish Department building of the university that I woke up from my sleep! I believe that God saw my earnest desire to keep praying in spite of an impossible medical school schedule.

Principle No. 6: Prayer Must Continue Both in Troubled Times and in Times of Peace

Why do we wait for trouble before we pray? Would you take someone as a serious friend if he only called you when he was in serious trouble? In times of peace, he had no time for you. God is looking for someone who will fellowship with him in both good and bad times.

The more I preach, the better I become at preaching. The more you pray, the better you will become at prayer. In times of crises, you will find yourself rising up to the occasion and delivering powerful prayers that bring results.

Principle No. 7: Every Nation Needs Lots of Prayer and Prayerful Leaders

There is no doubt that the world is ruled by wicked spirits in high places. The earth is covered with human beings at war with each other on a daily basis. Famine, war, epidemics and disasters abound! You just have to keep your eyes on the international news and you will hear about another major disaster.

Dictators of all kinds abound in many nations. Like snakes, which shed their skin, many dictators of yesteryears have a new "Democratic look" but are still tyrants and despots at heart. Many national leaders are actually under the influence of evil spirits, and that makes them do the

things they do. They cling to power instead of honorably allowing others to have a chance at leadership. Like vampires, they drink the blood of the nation's wealth and stack it away in secret places.

Charismatic leaders like Hitler lead entire nations into initial prosperity, and then eventual destruction through war. I always remember how things changed in South Africa after President DeKlerk replaced President Botha. A new leader led to the release of Nelson Mandela and the end of apartheid. It is important for us to pray for these leaders so that our nation will prosper. The right person at the helm of affairs will make a lot of difference to our nation. I believe that the presence of a prayerful person like Daniel made a lot of difference to that nation.

Principle No. 8: It is Important to Pray for Long Periods of Time

Years ago, the only prayers I knew about were those that the priests read out to us in church. The longest I could pray was thirty to forty seconds and that was when I recited the Lord's prayer. There were three prayers I knew how to pray: The Lord's Prayer, Hail Mary and a Prayer to the Angel of God! However, as I grew in the Lord I learnt how to pray for myself. I can now pray for several hours at a time.

I always remember the first time I prayed for three hours. I was a student in Achimota School (Prince of Wales College). I was in the midst of a crisis and I needed the intervention of the Lord. I can also remember the first time I prayed for seven hours. I was a sixth former in the same Achimota School. I prayed from 10 a.m. to 5 p.m. I enjoy praying for long hours.

Praying for thirty minutes is almost like no prayer to me. Do not misunderstand me; I am not saying that God does not hear short prayers. I am saying that I have developed the art of praying for long hours like Jesus did. Jesus prayed for three hours in the garden of Gethsemane.

And he went a little farther, and fell on his face, and prayed... And he cometh unto the disciples, and findeth them asleep, and saith unto Peter, WHAT, COULD YE NOT WATCH WITH ME ONE HOUR? He went away again the second time, and prayed... And he came and found them asleep again: for their eyes were heavy. And he left them, and went away again, and prayed the third time, saying the same words.

Matthew 26:39,40,42-44

In this Scripture, Jesus was surprised that the disciples could not pray for one hour.

And he cometh unto the disciples, and findeth them asleep, and saith unto Peter, What, could ye not watch with me one hour?

Matthew 26:40

Jesus prayed all night before he chose his disciples.

And it came to pass in those days, that he went out into a mountain to pray, and continued all night in prayer to God. And when it was day, he called unto him his disciples: and of them he chose twelve, whom also he named apostles;

Luke 6:12,13

Long prayer may not be an explicit instruction in the Bible, but it is implicit throughout the Word. In later chapters I will teach you what to pray about when you decide to pray for long hours.

Principle No. 9: It is Important to Enter Your Closet for Effective Prayer

Many Christians can only pray when they are in a group. They cannot stay in a room on their own and pray for one hour. That is a great handicap. **There is a difference between praying alone and praying with a group of people.** Both types of prayer are important. If you can pray for three hours on your own then you can pray for six hours with other people. It is easier to pray in a group. Each time, you expand your ability to pray alone, you are expanding your ability to chalk great achievements in prayer.

Principle No. 10: Everyone Must Develop the Ability and the Formulae for Praying Four Times a Day

There are four important times to pray: morning, afternoon, evening and all-the-time.

Jesus prayed in the morning and so do I.

And in the morning, rising up a great while before day, he went out, and departed into a solitary place, and there prayed.

Mark 1:35

What is so important about morning prayer? Prayer in the morning is very good because you meet God before you meet the devil. You meet God before you meet the circumstances of life. God anoints you to overcome every mountain that you will encounter in your life.

Prayer in the afternoon signifies prayer in the midst of activities.

And when he had sent them away, he departed into a mountain to pray.

Mark 6:46

When you pray in the afternoon, it signifies that in the heat of the day and in the thick of the battle, you recognize God as the most important force in your life. God will bless you for afternoon prayer. I see you praying in the afternoon!

You can take a little time off your lunch break and pray. That prayer will do you more good than a plate of rice will!

It is also important to pray in the evenings. When the Bible says "watch and pray", it does not mean keep your eyes open when you pray. What it actually means is, stay awake and pray.

And it came to pass in those days, that he went out into a mountain to pray, and continued all night in prayer to God.

Luke 6:12

There is something about praying in the night that is different from praying during the day. It is a very different experience. I have heard stories that witches are very active around 2 a.m. in the night. *Perhaps when you pray in the night you are tackling the forces of darkness in a different way.* After all, they are called the forces of darkness (night).

The fourth important time to pray is "all-the-time"

Pray without ceasing.

1 Thessalonians 5:17

Prayer is intended to be a never-ending stream of communication with your Heavenly Father. He has given us the baptism of the Holy Spirit and the gift of speaking in tongues. I pray all the time. My wife tells me that sometimes I pray in my sleep!

Pray without ceasing.

1 Thessalonians 5:17

You can pray on the bus and on your way to work. You can pray softly to yourself when you are in the office. You can pray when you are in the shower. God is happy when His children are constantly in touch with Him.

I have a friend whose wife calls him on his mobile phone at least seven times a day. I have been in meetings with him when he had received not less that four calls from his wife. Nothing important, she was just keeping in touch! I think it is a nice thing. She phones without ceasing!

I see you praying without ceasing! I see you praying in the morning and in the evening! God is changing your life because of your new found prayer life! Your marriage, business and ministry will never be the same by the time you finish reading this book!

When, like Daniel, you decide to pray for long hours, you will discover that you will need to have a pattern or a formula for prayer. You need something that will guide you in your prayer life. In these next chapters, we will study the formulae for prayer.

Daniel's Principles of Prayer

- ■ Prayer is very important.

- ■ No one is ever too busy, too blessed or too successful to pray.

- ■ Prayer is the source of our power and protection.

- ■ Prayer is important in acquiring and sustaining the blessings of God.

- ■ For prayer to be effective, it must be habitual.

- ■ Prayer must continue both in troubled times and in times of peace.

- Every nation needs lots of prayer and prayerful leaders.

- It is important to pray for long periods of time.

- It is important to enter your closet for effective prayer.

- Everyone must develop the ability and the formulae for praying four times a day.

Chapter 2

The Timothy Prayer Formula

S omeone may ask, "What do I pray about for one whole hour? I do not have anything to say after five minutes!" I have had that experience before. Many Christians begin to look at their watches after one and a half minutes of prayer. Somehow, it seems there is nothing left to say. That is why you need a prayer formula.

What is a prayer formula? A prayer formula is something that gives you guidelines for prayer. When you read through the Bible, you will discover exactly what to pray about. I call these *prayer formulae.* I want to share with you a few of these to help you develop a powerful prayer life.

The Timothy Prayer

The Timothy prayer is a prayer that I have used many times. Here it goes:

I exhort therefore, that, first of all, supplications, prayers, intercessions, and giving of thanks, be made for all men; For kings, and for all that are in authority; that we may lead a quiet and peaceable life in all godliness and honesty. For this is good and acceptable in the sight of God our Saviour;

1 Timothy 2:1-3

This Scripture tells us the types of prayers we must pray, and whom we must pray for. It tells us to pray for all men and specifically for leaders; Heads of State and anyone who has some form of authority over our lives. This prayer formula does not teach us to curse our leaders or to wish them evil.

There are four types of prayers we are to offer for each person who is in authority: supplications, prayers, intercessions and giving of thanks. We are to take each leader and pray that God would supply their needs. We are to thank God for their lives. We are to pray generally for them. Finally, we are to intercede for them.

Anyone who prays this "Timothian" prayer will experience four blessings from the Lord. You will experience a quiet life, a peaceful life, a godly life and an honest life. Whoever you are, this prayer formula can apply to you. There is someone, who has some form of authority over your life.

In my country, we have a President and a parliament who rule in the affairs of our nation. One way or the other, the decisions they take affect everyone. Recently, the entire country experienced a major power crisis which led to severe power rationing. Our church activities were greatly affected. Whether we liked it or not, the decisions taken by those in charge of electricity generation were affecting us.

The Word of God says that prayer for our leaders is important if we want to continue living a godly life.

Years ago, I was going to a broadcasting station to do a recording with a Christian group. When I got to a place called Danquah Circle, I realized that there was not a single car or human being in sight even though this is normally a very busy area. When I heard the sound of heavy artillery, I decided to retreat to my home for my dear life's sake. I later found out that there had been a military takeover in the capital city of Accra. Some soldiers had decided to overthrow the military government of the day. Because of this coup d'etat, our Christian recording for television could not take place. Once again, we could not lead our godly lives because of instability in our nation's leadership.

Dear friends, where we do not have peace and stability the work of God will not go on. As I write this book, I have a pastor and a church in Freetown, Sierra Leone. I keep watching the news to see what is going on there. I heard a new war was starting there. If there is war over there, I cannot keep a pastor stationed there. How will I explain to the pastor's wife if something happens to him?

Kings and Princes

There are certain parts of Africa which are no-go zones. Missionary work and church work have grounded to a halt because it is not safe to be there. This is why God tells us to pray for kings and people in authority.

If you study Ezekiel, you will find out that although there was a King of Tyrus in the natural, there was also a King of Tyrus in the spiritual.

Son of man, say unto the prince of Tyrus...Son of man, take up a lamentation upon the king of Tyrus...

Ezekiel 28:2,12

It is clear that this prince of Tyrus is a human being because it says,

...thou art a man and not God, though thou set thine heart as the heart of God...

Ezekiel 28:2

However, in verse twelve of the same chapter, the Bible says,

Son of man take up a lamentation upon the king of Tyrus...

Ezekiel 28:12

This time the Bible says,

Thou hast been in Eden the garden of God...

Ezekiel 28:13

It continues in verse 14,

Thou art the anointed cherub [angelic being]...

Ezekiel 28:14

This king of Tyrus was not a man; he was an angelic being. I am convinced that there are evil spirits that rule the nations. Tyrus had a supernatural being that ruled its affairs. This fellow was also called the king of Tyrus. Why was he called the king of Tyrus? Because he actually governed and ruled in Tyrus!

When Jesus was tempted in the wilderness, one of the offers that Satan made to him was to give him all of the kingdoms of the world. If Satan could not have given the kingdoms of the world to Jesus, it would not have been a temptation. It was a real temptation to Jesus because Satan was actually the one in control of the kingdoms of the world. You cannot give something that you do not have!

You and I can see that the world is headed towards eventual annihilation. There will probably be a nuclear war one-day. Some people sing, *"He's got the whole world in His hands."* I do not believe that is true. If the Lord had the whole world in His hands, the world would not be in the mess that it is in. If Jesus was ruling this world, there would not be wars in Rwanda, Burundi, Angola, Ethiopia, Eritrea, Central African Republic, Liberia, Sierra Leone, Democratic Republic of Congo, Congo Brazzaville, Bosnia, Afghanistan, Israel, Palestine and the list goes on!

If Jesus were in control of this world there would not be such injustice and wickedness throughout the world. The Bible tells us clearly that Satan is the god of this world.

In whom the god of this world hath blinded the minds of them which believe not, lest the light of the glorious gospel of Christ, who is the image of God, should shine on them.

2 Corinthians 4:4

For some reason, Satan seems to have legal control over the nations of this earth. **Before God can intervene in the affairs of men, He has to be invited by a legitimate citizen**

of this world. You and I are legitimate members of the world community. If the Lord gets involved without a legal invitation, Satan can accuse Him of the crime of illegal takeovers, such as happened with Iraq and Kuwait.

God is waiting for our invitation through prayer. When we invite Him to build our nations in freedom, justice and peace, He will do just that. Whenever Christians pray for leaders, there is a change.

Once, Abraham's wife was illegally taken by the King of the day. God appeared to the king called Abimelech, and said, "You are a dead man. You have taken somebody's wife to be your own." The king was scared; he thought he was going to die. But God told him: "Tell Abraham to pray for you."

Now therefore restore the man his wife; for he is a prophet, and he [Abraham] shall pray for thee, and thou shalt live: and if thou restore her not, know thou that thou shalt surely die, thou, and all that are thine.

Genesis 20:7

Why did God not deliver Abimelech right away? After all, He knew about the prayer that Abraham was going to pray. But no, God has to wait for the invitation of men before getting involved in the affairs of this world.

There are three main reasons why we need to pray for those in authority. First, we have to pray that the decisions of the nation will not be based on selfish and political desires only. The second reason is that the nature of all men is to grab and take as much as they can. We have to pray against corruption. Thirdly, we must pray for peace and freedom so that we may go about our Christian duties without any hindrance.

We need to pray that our leaders will truly love the nation. How can you know when a leader loves the nation?

For he loveth our nation and hath built us a synagogue.

Luke 7:5

When a leader loves the nation, he will build the nation and not his personal wealth.

You Must Pray for Your Boss

If you do not pray for those who have authority over you, your life may become frustrated. The Bible tells us that the heart of the king is in the hand of the Lord, and He turns it whichever way he wants.

The king's heart is in the hand of The Lord, as the rivers of water: he turneth it whithersoever he will.

Proverbs 21:1

In Genesis chapter 40, you will find a very interesting story. There was a king who had a butler and a baker. The butler was in charge of everything in the home. The baker made biscuits, cakes and pies that the king enjoyed eating. Something happened in the workplace that made the king angry with both the butler and the baker. In his wrath, he had them thrown into prison.

Whilst there, each of them had a dream which Joseph (who had been wrongfully imprisoned) interpreted. He predicted that the butler would be re-instated and the baker would lose his life.

Now, understand that both the butler and the baker were in trouble. Their very lives depended on the one they had displeased. Everything depended on how Pharaoh thought. Depending on his decision, someone would live or die. In this particular case, the baker died, just as Joseph predicted.

There are times when your life depends on what someone thinks about you. The more you pray Timothy's prayer, the more favorable the thoughts of your boss will be towards you. I see you having favor in all that you do! I see the heart of the king having mercy on you!

Many young people must pray for their fathers in order to have the favour of God. I remember when I was in the university, I asked my father for a car. I realized that my father was spending a lot of money on horse racing. You see, my father had one of the largest horseracing stables in the country. He employed many people and bought horses from all over West Africa. I thought to myself, "If my father wants to, he can buy a brand new car for me."

One day, my father decided to buy a car for me. My prayers for him made the Lord turn his heart in my favor. I received a brand new car when I was in fifth year medical school. I rejoiced and used that car for the glory of God. I was the first church member of Lighthouse Chapel International to own a car. My car became the church bus and the church taxi. And I was happy to do it, because I knew that the Lord had provided.

God can bless you through those who are in authority over you. As you pray for them, God will give you favor! Things are changing in your favor! I see God turning the heart of every king in your life! They will not decide to kill you anymore. They will decide that you must live! I see many blessings rising up to embrace you! **As you pray for fathers, bosses and presidents, you will experience only godliness, peace and quietness.**

From today, every wife that prays for her husband will experience quietness in her house! From now on, your "unbeliever" husband will allow you to go to church!

He will not stop you from going for all-night prayer meetings. He will not oppose your Christian life anymore because you are praying for him!

Chapter 3

The Ephesians Prayer Formula

Wherefore I also, after I heard of your faith in the Lord Jesus, and love unto all the saints, Cease not to give thanks for you, making mention of you in my prayers; That the God of our Lord Jesus Christ, the Father of glory, may give unto you the spirit of wisdom and revelation in the knowledge of him: The eyes of your understanding being enlightened; that ye may know what is the hope of his calling, and what the riches of the glory of his inheritance in the saints, And what is the exceeding greatness of his power to us-ward who believe, according to the working of his mighty power, Which he wrought in Christ, when he raised him from the dead, and set him at his own right hand in the Heavenly places, Far above all principality, and power, and might,

and dominion, and every name that is named, not only in this world, but also in that which is to come: And hath put all things under his feet, and gave him to be the head over all things to the church, Which is his body, the fulness of him that filleth all in all.

Ephesians 1:15-23

Many people just gloss over Ephesians chapter one. They think it is too complicated to understand. However, God reveals to us a major formula for prayer in this chapter. I call it the *Ephesians prayer formula*. The Ephesians prayer formula has six important steps.

- The 1st step is to give thanks with a grateful heart.

- The 2nd step is to pray for wisdom and revelation in the knowledge of him.

- The 3rd step is to pray for the eyes of your understanding to be enlightened.

- The 4th step is to pray to know your calling and the hope of your calling.

- The 5th step is to pray to know the riches of the inheritance of the saints.

- The 6th step is to pray to know the power of God.

1. Give Thanks

Cease not to GIVE THANKS for you...

Ephesians 1:16

First of all, you must give thanks. Many people have become hardened and ungrateful. It is nice when you meet a few grateful people among the masses of ungrateful people in the world! The first thing to do therefore, under this prayer formula, is to spend quality time thanking the Lord in prayer. Thank Him for His goodness and mercies, thank Him for His protection, thank Him for His provision— the list is endless!

2. Cry to the Lord for Revelation

The second important step is to cry out to the Lord for revelation. This is one of my favorite prayer topics. *You may know something, but until it is revealed to you in a deeper way, you do not really know it!* There is a difference between "head" knowledge and "revelation" knowledge.

Revelation Knowledge

That the God of our Lord Jesus Christ, the Father of glory, may give unto you the SPIRIT OF WISDOM AND REVELATION IN THE KNOWLEDGE OF HIM.

Ephesians 1:17

I have always known that it is dangerous to drive very fast. I have seen large billboards that declare, *"The speed that thrills is the speed that kills."* One day I travelled to Tamale in the northern region of Ghana. I was driving at over 120 kilometers per hour when suddenly a cyclist crossed my path. I soon found myself somersaulting in the air. After that experience, I had revelation knowledge about driving too fast!

I remember one night I was on a highway driving at about eighty kilometres per hour when suddenly three cars overtook me with the speed of a bullet. Such was their speed that it looked as though my car was stationary. I smiled and thought to myself, *"There was a time no car ever overtook me on a highway.* These people do not have revelation knowledge." What I had experienced had given me a deeper understanding of the knowledge about over-speeding. We call this type of knowledge - revelation knowledge.

There is a difference between knowing something and having a revelation about it. The more I pray for revelation, the more I understand the Word of God. The cardinal thing that has taken me forward in my walk with God has been the revelation I have had in His Word. When you have had a revelation, you change. **The cardinal sign of revelation is a change in your life.**

Every year I have a deeper and progressive revelation of God and His Word. If you are a pastor, spend hours praying for wisdom and revelation. God anoints people who know Him. When I say know Him, I am talking about having a revelation of God through His Word. The things I am sharing with you in this book are things I know by revelation. They are more real to me than facts from a history book.

I often tell my lay pastors that this life is short and that the only thing worth doing is the work of the ministry. Jesus himself said to "lay up for yourself treasures in Heaven". The revelation of this Scripture is deep in my heart. But most people do not have a revelation of it. Although many people know this Scripture, it has not been revealed to them. That is why I could give up a lucrative medical career for the ministry. I believe I will one day reap great Heavenly rewards which are more valuable than any amount of money.

That is why I could give up a quiet life of wealth and privacy in exchange for a public, often criticized role of being a spiritual leader. I have a revelation of the truth, that, "Vanity of vanity...all is vanity" (Ecclesiastes 1:2).

The Lawyer Received Revelation

I once visited a dying man in the hospital. He was a young and successful lawyer struck down in the midst of his years with a deadly disease. I will never forget something he said to us; "If God would raise me up from this bed I will serve Him. Even if it means becoming a full-time preacher."

As this man lay dying, he realized how futile everything in this world really was. He suddenly had revelation knowledge about many things that are written in the Bible. Somehow we read the Bible but we do not get the revelation of it. When you pray for the Spirit of Revelation, things which you have read over and over will come alive to you in a different way.

3. Pray for Understanding

The EYES OF YOUR UNDERSTANDING BEING ENLIGHTENED; that ye may know what is the hope of his calling, and what the riches of the glory of his inheritance in the saints...

Ephesians 1:18

The next step in the Ephesians prayer formula is to pray for understanding. When you have understanding, you know why you should obey the Word of God. I often pray for the Spirit of understanding. When you have understanding, it helps you to obey God's instructions. Because I ask for understanding, God often shows me many deep things in His Word.

That is why I can preach *"Twenty-five Reasons Why We Should Have a Mega Church"*. I teach *"Twenty Reasons why Poverty is a Curse"*. I once taught, *"Fifty-five Reasons why we Should Win Souls"*. Believe it or not, each of those

28

reasons were different. *"Ten Reasons Why We Should Not Commit Fornication"*, *"Ten Reasons Why You Should Love Your Husband"*. When you have the Spirit of understanding you will know why God is speaking to you the way He is.

There are many Christian wives who are unwilling to do their duties in their marriage. The reason is, they do not have an understanding about the duties of a wife. I notice how the revelation of the importance of the duties of a wife comes alive when a woman is struck with the reality of an adulterous husband.

4. Pray About Your Calling

The eyes of your understanding being enlightened; that ye may know what is the HOPE OF HIS CALLING, and what the riches of the glory of his inheritance in the saints...

Ephesians 1:18

The 4th step in the Ephesian prayer formula is to pray about your calling. Every Christian is called to a ministry.

For we are his workmanship, created in Christ Jesus unto good works, which God hath before ordained that we should walk in them.

Ephesians 2:10

Christians were not recreated for nothing. God intends for every one of us to fulfil our divine call. We are called to do good works. We are called to be unmovable, steadfast, always abounding in the work of the Lord.

I watch modern-day Christians attend service after service. Christianity has become a kind of ritual for many people.

They just attend church, sing songs and listen to a thirty-minute sermon. But there is more to the calling of God than that.

When I became a Christian, I joined a vibrant ministry that went around preaching the Word. To me, Christianity has always been an experience of soul-winning and establishing other Christians in the Lord.

The Taxi Driver Did Not Believe Me!

I was once chatting with a taxi driver in London. He asked me where I was coming from. I told him, "I've just flown in from Amsterdam."

He said, "Oh, there are a lot of prostitutes there; did you have a good time?"

I answered, "Oh no! I'm a Christian. We don't live like that!"

He exclaimed, "Are you sure Christians don't do that? Do you really believe that stuff? Do you actually believe in Heaven?"

He went on, "If Heaven is really so nice then why don't we all commit suicide and go there right now."

Unfortunately I had got to the end of my journey and could not explain the hope (the reason) of my calling as a Christian. This taxi driver brought up a very valid point. **If we are all just waiting to enter Heaven, why not just go there right away?**

The answer is simple: Christians are not expected to kill themselves! Christians have an important calling to save souls and to establish people in the Lord.

We cannot just rush to Heaven now! The hope (reason) for our calling is to bear fruit and win souls in this life. That is why we are still here and have not left for Heaven yet. According to Revelations 14:13, your works will follow you into Heaven.

...Blessed are the dead which die in the Lord from henceforth: Yea, saith the Spirit, that they may rest from their labours; and their works do follow them.

Revelations 14:13

What you do on earth will determine how your stay in Heaven will be like. If you know why Christ has saved you, you will have a lot to do for him here on earth.

5. To Know the Riches of Your Inheritance in Christ

The eyes of your understanding being enlightened; that ye may know what is the hope of his calling, and what the RICHES OF THE GLORY OF HIS INHERITANCE IN THE SAINTS...

Ephesians 1:18

The next step is to know the riches of our inheritance in Christ. This means we need to know what we have inherited as Christians.

When my father died, he left properties for his children. A few months after he died, we assembled in Court to listen to the reading of his will. We all wanted to know what the riches of our inheritance were. We took the time to find out what we had inherited. I did not know what my father had given to me. I had to go to the Court to find out for myself.

It is sad to say that many Christians do not bother to find out what God has in store for them. When you begin to discover what God has in store for you, you will be amazed. **We need to pray to know what God has given to us.**

Are We Supposed to Be Poor?

Many people think that Christians are supposed to be poor. They think that pastors, in particular, are supposed to be impoverished. There are people who want ministers to come crawling to their doorsteps to beg for a tin of sardines and a loaf of bread. Is this what we have inherited from our Heavenly Father? No, certainly not!

I do not intend to be poor just because I am a minister! I am sorry if that offends you, but I cannot see it in my Bible. Apostle Peter wanted to find out how he would benefit from following Christ, so he asked,

Lo, we have left all, and followed thee…

Mark 10:28

In other words, how do we benefit from serving you? Jesus answered him clearly. That answer applies to all of us,

…There is no man that hath left house, or brethren, or sisters, or father, or mother, or wife, or children, or lands, for my sake, and the gospel's. But he shall receive an hundredfold now in this time, houses, and brethren, and sisters, and mothers, and children, and lands, with persecutions; and in the world to come eternal life.

Mark 10:29, 30

The heritage of Christians and ministers is not lack and poverty. But if you do not find out or pray about it you will live in the darkness of that deception all the days of your life.

6. To Know the Greatness of God's Power

And what is the EXCEEDING GREATNESS of his power to us-ward who believe, according to the working of his mighty power...

Ephesians 1:19

The last step of the Ephesians prayer formula is to pray to know the greatness of God's power. There are certain Christians who do not want anything to do with the power of God. In the last days, the Bible teaches that some people will have a form of godliness but will deny the reality of the power of the Gospel (2 Timothy 3:5).

One of the things you need to pray about is to know the power of the Holy Spirit. **There are two types of churches in the world: teaching churches and power churches.** Some churches emphasize the teaching and have nothing to do with the power of God. That is a mistake! You cannot take away miracles from the Bible. Without the miracles of the Bible all we are left with is philosophical literature.

It is because people do not believe in the power, that they are frightened by weird looking witches and fetish priests. We need to pray for the power until we experience it. You will not taste of God's power unless you pray for it! Thank God for nice teachings on Sunday. Thank God for good administration. However, there is a power dimension to Christianity and God wants you to experience it too.

Chapter 4

The Lord's Prayer Formula

After this manner therefore pray ye: Our Father which art in Heaven, Hallowed be thy name. Thy kingdom come. Thy will be done in earth, as it is in Heaven. Give us this day our daily bread. And forgive us our debts, as we forgive our debtors. And lead us not into temptation, but deliver us from evil: For thine is the kingdom, and the power, and the glory, for ever. Amen.

Matthew 6:9-13

One of the things that struck the disciples about the Lord Jesus was His ability to pray for long hours. They wanted to know what strategy, formula or trick He used in order to stay in prayer for such long hours.

That is why they approached Him and said, "Lord, teach us how to pray." They needed to have a sort of guideline for their prayer lives. Jesus sat them down and gave them eight steps to enhance their personal prayer lives.

1. Give Thanks and Worship the Lord

Our Father which art in Heaven, Hallowed be thy name.

Matthew 6:9

Jesus taught us that the first step is to say thank you and to worship the Lord. The first thing to do in this prayer formula is to spend time giving thanks to the Lord. For most people thanksgiving lasts for approximately forty-five seconds.

However, we need to be grateful to the Lord for all that He has done for us. Thank Him for allowing you to see that day. Many people die everyday, it could have been you. The fact that you are alive is a miracle. Thank Him for your pastor and your church.

Thank Him that you can read this book. I have members in my Bible school who cannot write. During the classes, they have to record what is said on tape. They simply do not have the ability to read or write. I thank God for the fact that I am in the ministry. The fact that you are reading my book is a miracle of God.

Some people can only see problems. God is touching your eyes right now! He is opening your eyes to see His blessings all around. In this first step of prayer, you must thank the Lord for what He has done for you.

A Sad Visit

I recently visited a friend of mine. He lived virtually on the street. He had become a drug addict, and he had no food or money. As I took some money out of my pocket to give to him, tears welled up in my eyes. I thought of how pathetic this young man's condition was. I realized that it could have been me. Somehow, by the grace of God I had come to know the Lord. I could have been smoking marijuana. After all, I saw many people doing it when I was younger. I could have been dead and buried long ago.

I have been in near-fatal car crashes. I have been in planes that almost collided with other planes on the runway. On two different occasions, I have been in aircrafts that landed and had to do an emergency takeoff in order to avoid a collision on the runway. But I am still here and I know I have something to thank God for.

My friends, if you cannot find something to thank God for, for at least ten minutes, then you have an ungrateful spirit. This first step of the Lord's Prayer Formula should last about ten minutes.

2. Pray for the Kingdom of God to Come

Thy kingdom come...

Matthew 6:10

The second important step is to pray for the kingdom of God to come. This step is my favourite step. I can spend three hours here. But if you do not have much time, you can spend just ten minutes on this. Please note here that the order is very important. The first thing is to pray for the church and the kingdom. Ask God to bless the church.

36

I teach my children to pray for church growth all the time. When the church is growing, it is an indication that more people are being saved everyday. Everybody is developing his personal kingdom. People are developing their financial strength. Most people do not really care about the church. Every Christian must first pray for the church to develop and grow.

Pray for your pastors instead of criticizing them. Men of God are human beings just like you. Pastors make so many mistakes everyday. Unfortunately, our mistakes are often publicized. Pray that God will protect His leaders from attacks of all sorts.

3. God's Will Be Done

...Thy will be done in earth as it is in Heaven.

Matthew 6:10

The third step is to pray for the will of God to be done. This can also take another ten minutes. *Anyone who prays that God's will should be done in his life, cares for himself.* If you love yourself, pray that the will of God be done in your life. I have come to believe that God's will is better than my will or anybody else's will. Nobody knows the future, but God knows what He has in store for you.

Jesus prayed for three hours in the garden of Gethsemane that the will of God be done. After you have prayed this prayer you can relax and allow events to unfold. When Judas and the Pharisees came to arrest Christ, he did not resist them. He believed and accepted that the events that were happening were the will of God, and indeed they were. Those events were leading him to his greatest victory over Satan.

37

If you want to have peace and confidence in this life, spend time praying that the will of God comes to pass in your life.

My Evening Prayer

Many years ago, I was a young medical student. I had no idea that I would be where I am today. In 1985, during the first term of my third year, I spent many hours praying that the will of God be done. Our school campus was near the Atlantic Ocean. Every night at 10 p.m. I went along with four other friends to the beach. I clearly remember standing on the rocks and the sand praying, "O Lord, let thy will be done."

As I stood on the dark shores of Ghana, I remembered how missionaries came to our nation and sacrificed their lives. I lifted up my hands on the beach and said, "Use me Lord. Let your will be done." I cried to the Lord and said, "You brought me here. I do not know the future. Whatever you want to be done, let it come to pass." I believe that today I am walking in the answers of those prayers. For several weeks, I prayed those same prayers.

Begin to spend time praying to God for His will to be done. Do you think the will of God will happen naturally? Certainly not! If it was going to happen naturally why would you have to spend time praying about it? The very fact that Jesus taught us to pray about it means that it is not automatic that the will of God will happen.

I see your future unfolding in a positive way! I see God lifting you up as you pray about His will! I see you marrying the right person as you spend time praying for the will of God to be done!

4. Our Daily Bread

Give us this day our daily bread.

Matthew 6:11

The next step is to pray for our daily bread. Jesus taught us to pray for our daily needs. That means we are to pray about our jobs, marriages and everything that concerns us.

Some years ago I felt I was too spiritual to marry. But no one can be more spiritual than God. Do not be too spiritual to ask God for your physical needs. Ask him for a house. Ask him for bread. Do you want a husband? God is granting him to you right now as you read this book. Pray to the Lord for yourself. Spend some minutes mentioning your needs to the Lord. If you spend another ten minutes asking the Lord for your daily needs, your life will change dramatically.

When it comes to prayer do not depend on anyone, depend on yourself. Do not expect somebody to pray for you. Many times, people who you think are praying for you are actually sleeping.

God is giving you a formula for prayer. Operate in it and walk in your blessings.

5. Pray for Forgiveness

And forgive us our debts, as we forgive our debtors.

Matthew 6:12

The next step is to pray for forgiveness. We all need forgiveness for our sins. There are two types of sins: sins of commission and sins of omission. We must be aware of our sinful nature as we approach the throne of grace.

Appropriate the blood of Jesus for yourself. Ask the Lord to see you only through the eyes of the blood.

One of the first sins of commission is the sin of the mouth: lying, flattery, backbiting, gossip, etc. Another arena for sin is the mind. Many of us have committed murder, adultery and stealing in our minds. Our minds are often polluted with sin. We must come before the Lord and pray for mercy. As we ask the Lord for mercy, we must search our hearts to see whether we have forgiven the people around us.

Sometimes I listen to the way people condemn those who have made mistakes. It makes me sad! Are we not all human? Are we not all subject to the same temptations? Is it not by the grace of God that we survive?

When we come to this part of the prayer, we must correct any judgmental or arrogant attitudes.

One of the important sins to confess is the sin of omission. There are people who go to Hell because a neighbour did not witness to them. There are friends who die and go to hell because we never told them about Christ. As we come before the throne, God sees all our mistakes. If we act as though we are perfect, we deceive ourselves

and the truth is not in us. Spend another ten minutes asking the Lord to have mercy on your life.

6. Pray Against Temptation

And lead us not into temptation...

Matthew 6:13

The next important step in The Lord's Prayer Formula is to pray against temptation. We are all human beings. When I hear of great men of God falling, I become so frightened. I wonder about myself. Many times I just pray that I will just make it safely to Heaven. It is important for you to pray against temptations in your life. You may not know, but prayer strengthens you against temptations.

Fasting Without Prayer is Dieting

On the night of betrayal, Jesus gave the disciples an eternal command, "Pray in case you fall into a temptation." Many years ago, I remember fasting for three days. By the third day, I was so weak that I could not rise out of the bed. This was the first time I had fasted for three days without any food at all. Because we had not prayed, I was almost unconscious.

Some months later I decided to try this fast again. This time I decided to wake up at 4 a.m. and spend a couple of hours in prayer before the day began. By the third day of the fast, I felt as though I had had something to eat. There was a great difference between the two fasts. I had such strength because I had been more prayerful.

My Christian friend, prayer is a supernatural act and provides strength even when your flesh is weak. Spend about twenty minutes praying against temptations in your life.

7. Pray that God Delivers You From Evil

...deliver us from evil...

Matthew 6:13

The seventh step is to pray that God should deliver you from evil. It is important for you to pray against the evils in this world. Cover yourself with the blood of Jesus. In the days of Israel, they would sprinkle the blood of lambs over the lintels and doorposts. This was to prevent any evil from coming into the home. We are to do the same thing now but in a spiritual way.

And they shall take of the blood, and strike it on the two side posts and on the upper door post...aND WHEN I SEE THE BLOOD, I WILL PASS OVER YOU...

Exodus 12:7,13

How do you sprinkle the blood? You sprinkle the blood of Jesus with your words. Apply the blood of Jesus over every part of your home and family. Place an injunction over every flying witch. Declare that your household is a no-fly-zone for every witch, wizard or evil presence. Cancel every enchantment, spell, charm or lamentation that has been taken up against you. Declare that you will live and not die. Bind Satan and his agents. Have faith in God. Command angelic beings and the forces of Heaven to be on guard around you. God will keep you as you pray against evil in your life.

8. Thank Him and Give Him Glory

...For thine is the kingdom, and the power, and the glory, for ever. Amen.

Matthew 6:13

The final thing to do in The Lord's Prayer Formula is to thank Him and to give Him glory. For thine is the kingdom, the power and the glory. Thank Him over and over. Declare that He is more powerful than the walls of opposition in your life. Declare that every mountain of impossibility is possible because of His power and His glory.

Lift up your hands and speak about his glorious power in your life. Declare that every serpentine agenda for your life cannot happen because of the power, kingdom and the glory of God. Thank Jehovah that He has time for you to listen to your prayer. Thank Him that it is well with your soul. Thank Him that it is well with you.

If you follow these steps, you will have at least an hour and half of effective and fruitful prayer everyday.

It is my prayer that these strategies for prayer will revolutionalize your spiritual life. May you move into greater heights in God's kingdom, as you apply the principles in this book.

Other Best-Selling Books by Dag Heward-Mills:

*Loyalty and Disloyalty

Leaders and Loyalty

Transform Your Pastoral Ministry

The Art of Leadership

Model Marriage

Church Planting

*The Megachurch

*Lay People and the Ministry

*These titles are also available in Spanish and French. Information about other foreign translations of some of the titles above may be obtained by writing to our address.